W9-BBM-411

# HIPPOS in the NIGHT

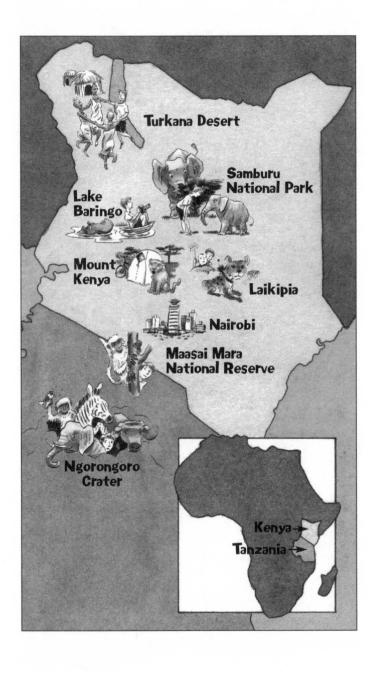

Turkana Desert

Samburu National Park

Lake Baringo

Mount Kenya

Laikipia

Nairobi

Maasai Mara National Reserve

Ngorongoro Crater

Kenya→

Tanzania→

Autobiographical Adventures in Africa

# HIPPOS
# in the NIGHT

# Christina Allen

### Illustrations by
# Rob Shepperson

HarperCollins*Publishers*

Photo credits: pages 23, 36, 77, and 90, © 1998 by Christina Allen;
page 53, © 1998 by Dan Buettner;
pages 13, 61, 92, and 108, © 1998 by Beth Wald/Aurora.
All rights reserved.

Hippos in the Night
Text copyright © 2003 by Christina Allen
Illustrations copyright © 2003 by Rob Shepperson
Printed in the United States of America.
For information address HarperCollins Children's Books,
a division of HarperCollins Publishers, 1350 Avenue of the Americas,
New York, NY 10019.
www.harperchildrens.com

Library of Congress Cataloging-in-Publication Data
Allen, Christina M.
    Hippos in the night : autobiographical adventures in Africa /
Christina Allen ; illustrations by Rob Shepperson.
       p.   cm.
    Summary: Biologist Christina Allen describes her adventures
in Africa, including watching the shadow of a hippo lurking
outside her tent, trying to ride a camel, and watching a dung
beetle in action.
    Contents: How I got there—My first wild animal sighting—
Lost—Tenting in hippo territory—Camel rides and baboon
friends—Meeting the Hadza tribe—Wild animal soup.
    ISBN 0-688-17826-X — ISBN 0-688-17827-8 (lib. bdg.)
    1. Endangered species—Africa—Juvenile literature. 2. Allen,
Christina M.—Journeys—Africa—Juvenile literature. 3. Africa—
Description and travel—Juvenile literature. [1. Endangered
species. 2. Zoology—Africa. 3. Allen, Christina M. 4. Africa—
Description and travel.] I. Shepperson, Rob, ill. II. Title.
QL84.6.A1 A58 2003
591.96—dc21                                              2002068735
                                                              CIP
                                                               AC

Typography by Amy Ryan
1  2  3  4  5  6  7  8  9  10

First Edition

*To my mom, Jane,
and dad, Jack,
who encouraged my curiosity
and love for nature,
and to Barbara,
who gave me a chance as a writer*

"To see ten thousand animals untamed . . .
is like scaling an unconquered mountain
for the first time, or like finding a forest
without roads or footpaths. . . .
You know then what you had always been told—
that the world once lived and grew
without adding machines and newsprint
and brick-walled streets and the tyranny of clocks."
—Beryl Markham
*West with the Night*

"I really do simply adore Kenya.
It is so wild, uncultivated, primitive,
mad, exciting, unpredictable. . . .
I am living in the Africa I have always longed for,
always felt stirring in my blood."
—from Jane Goodall's first letter home, 1957

# Contents

# 1. How I Got There

*Can you imagine . . .*

Trying to sleep with a munching, crunching hippo feeding inches from your head? Challenging a young baboon to a fight . . . by mistake? Waking up in the dark to the shattering roar of a lion just outside your tent? Playing football with huge, round loaves of elephant poop? Sniffing the soft, sweet fur behind a hyena's ear?

How do I get myself into these crazy situations with animals? I'm not exactly sure, but I think it has something to do with worms.

When I was two years old, my mom found me in the backyard laughing hysterically. I was pouring a huge jar of fishing worms all over my lap. Worms wriggled across my legs and squirmed in between my toes and fingers. My mom didn't say, "Christina, that is gross, yucky, icky!" Instead she just laughed and joined me. She's a biologist and thinks worms are cool, too.

When I was six, we moved to Alaska for my dad's job. "Just a year" turned into fifteen, and my lawyer father became a bush pilot, flying small planes into the wilderness. We spent most of our free time looking for wildlife. Flying over Cook Inlet, we would spot what looked like grains of rice floating in chocolate milk, then fly low to discover a pod of beluga whales. Arriving home, we wouldn't be surprised to find a moose snacking on winter cabbages in our garden. Sometimes a moose and her baby would camp out in our backyard for days! After they left, I would poke around their grassy bed. I learned that moose "nuggets" are round and dry, perfect for target practice on trees and rocks.

I was ten years old when I watched *Out of Africa* with my parents. In the dead of the Alaskan winter, I suddenly imagined myself flying over the hot, dry African grasslands, watching great herds of zebra and wildebeest. I pictured myself on safari, dressed all in tan, creeping dangerously close to photograph a herd of elephants. Throughout my teens I continued to dream of being on safari in Africa. I especially dreamed of seeing lions in the wild. Still, Africa seemed so far away that I never really thought I'd get there.

Science and biology were

my favorite subjects through grade school, high school, and college. I never tired of learning facts about animals and nature—even the parts most people think are gross. I loved the down-and-dirty aspects of animal anatomy and physiology and was fascinated by the cycles of birth, death, and decay that keep the environment in balance. In graduate school I was still playing with nuggets and worms, only I was doing it in the name of science! I studied wild animals in the Amazon rain forest to get a degree in tropical wildlife ecology and conservation. I would tromp around in the mud all day, following tapirs, stinky wild peccaries, and huge rodents, counting their tracks and collecting their poops. I was interested in the fruits, seeds, leaves, and other things the animals ate, and how their eating (and pooping) habits scattered seeds and helped to grow new trees in the rain forest. I was also concerned about people hunting the animals and cutting down the trees the animals depended on for food.

Before I finished graduate school, one of my teachers told me about a team of young scientists and adventurers that travels on worldwide expeditions called Quests. They explore the mystery of disappearing wildlife—then broadcast their findings to kids in classrooms all over America on the Internet! When I learned that the team often traveled by jeep and mountain bikes, I knew I had to go.

But how was I going to get on the team? I didn't even know how to mountain bike! So I started a crash course. I rented a bike to get myself in shape, but the first time I hit the trails, I encountered a big hill. I decided to go for it, but my technique was wrong. I went flying over the handlebars; then my bike went flying over me and landed right on top of my head, pinning me to the ground and breaking my helmet. My crash course was more crash than course, but I had learned my first lesson: to always, always wear a helmet.

I did everything I could think of to get on the team. I called the team members to tell them about people we could visit and theories we could explore; I sent recommendations from people who knew me and information about scientific research I'd done in the past. But after six months they were still unsure about taking me on. I was almost ready to give up, but something inside told me not to. As a last-ditch effort, I flew to Washington, D.C., to attend a big meeting with teachers. I followed the team around and talked to teachers about what we might encounter on Quests. I spoke about what I knew best, my research in the Amazon and the adventures I'd had there—from the thrill of seeing animals in the wild and learning something new about a little-known animal to such scary moments as falling ill with dengue fever in the middle of nowhere and being bitten by a poisonous snake.

I'm not sure if it was my stories or my persistence, but finally I was invited along as the team biologist! I felt so lucky, but even greater surprises were in store. As luck, or fate, would have it, kids and teachers voted for Africa as the next destination. My dream was coming true.

On AfricaQuest, we'd travel the length of East Africa's Great Rift Valley to meet with scientists and local people, gathering clues to the disappearing wildlife. Recent important research had come out, saying that many animals in Africa were dying off but that the causes were not clear. It said that some species, like elephants and Thompson's gazelles, had been reduced by more than half in just twenty years.

I knew next to nothing about the Great Rift

Valley but figured that studying about it might be safer than learning how to mountain bike. I found out that the Great Rift deserves its name. It's the longest rift, or crack, on the face of the earth! Four thousand miles long and in places almost two miles deep, the rift was created about five million years ago when two of the earth's plates collided. Along the rift extreme volcanic activity created mountains, craters, and ash layers deep enough to fill the crack. Without this thick ash layer, much of Kenya would be underwater today.

I could only imagine what it was like for the animals with ash and lava spewing all over the place. Sometimes the volcanoes would explode so suddenly that animals would get trapped in the lava flows and be instantly incinerated. People have actually found perfect shells of elephants, with every hair and wrinkle captured in hardened lava.

One of the most famous volcanoes, called Ngorongoro, grew with each lava flow until it was about twenty thousand feet high. In its center was a huge chamber of hot lava, or magma. One day the magma started to leak out and the enormous mountain collapsed, leaving the largest volcanic crater in the world. Today the crater has a big lake at the bottom and is one of the richest wildlife habitats in East Africa. When I read about the giant crater with the lake and all the wildlife, I felt I just had to see it. Seeing Ngorongoro Crater became my own personal goal, my reason for going to Kenya and Tanzania.

I was so busy getting ready that I completely forgot to be nervous. But a couple of days before we left, I started thinking of all the things that could go wrong, like *What if my bike breaks down and I get stranded all alone? What if a lion sees me as a tasty snack? What if I get sick?* I knew I should be excited, but suddenly I was scared.

Our day of departure came fast.

Scared or not, I stepped onto the plane and we took off.

This is the story of my African adventure.

# 2. My First Wild Animal Sighting

Flying into Africa is nothing like I'd expected. I thought I'd look out the plane window and see savannas below, full of elephants and giraffes. But as we break through the dirty gray clouds over Nairobi, Kenya's capital, I am shocked to see a big bustling city with cars and traffic and no animals anywhere in sight.

Walking off the plane, I am swarmed by people—men, women, and children all wanting me to buy something. After our fourteen-hour flight, I am exhausted. I look to my teammates for help, but each one is also surrounded by a small crowd. The men, who are selling safari tours and little carved wood animals, are saying "Safari? Safari?" and "Elephant? Giraffe?" The women, who are selling beaded jewelry, are saying "Good price." And the kids are saying "Hello? Hello? Please?" Some of them are smiling and just playing, testing to see what they can get from me, but a few have no shoes and look seriously in need.

The kids touch me the most, so I give them some money, pens, and paper. But there are kids everywhere I turn. I run out of things to give, and there are still so many in need, saying "Please?" and pointing to their mouths. I feel sad and overwhelmed, like I could never do enough to really help them.

Dizzy, hungry, and tired, I look around for my team members. Just then a huge man carrying a little boy cuts through the crowd and gently tells the other people to leave me alone. He introduces himself as Ndemo (en-DEM-o), and I am surprised to find that he already knows who I am. Apparently Ndemo has a friend in the U.S. who told him about our program. Knowing that the airport can be overwhelming for newcomers, Ndemo and his son traveled an hour from their home just to see if they could help. I feel humbled by this gesture, realizing most people at home, including myself, probably wouldn't go this far out of their way to help a stranger.

Shortly after meeting Ndemo, we are introduced to our guide, a friendly, shy young African man named Justus Erus. I like Justus immediately, and come to rely on his big smile, enthusiasm, and funny expressions. When he agrees with something, he says, "Fine! Yes, it can be fine!" Justus is a famous fossil hunter. He was recommended to us by a scientist who works with him at a fossil museum in Nairobi. Because Justus grew up in the Turkana tribe of northern Kenya, he is very familiar with both the city and the remote parts of Kenya. At the time, we were not aware that, in addition to being our guide, Justus would become invaluable to our team as a teacher, driver, translator, and close friend, helping us time and again through many challenging situations.

**A**fter the stress of the airport, we are excited to get going. We've all been eager to see the rugged expedition vehicle that we arranged to rent from a guy we met back in the States. I envisioned a large truck that would easily carry eight to ten people and all our bikes and gear over the roughest back roads to the remote places we'd visit in Kenya and Tanzania. I imagined the vehicle would become our home away from home, our safe haven, our passport to anywhere we needed to go. It grew in my mind's eye and became part of my dream of being on safari in Africa. But when we finally see the vehicle, I think, *This can't be it; this must be just something temporary until we can get our real overland expedition vehicle.*

Sitting in front of us is a Mitsubishi Pajero, a small SUV that's common in Africa and looks more like a car than an expedition vehicle! We look at one another, so disappointed, wondering how we're going to get ourselves

and all of our gear into this tiny thing with only four seats. There's a bike rack on the back, but no rack on the roof! We've already paid for the car and don't have enough money to get another one. Just as we are about to despair, Justus speaks up: "We can build a rack; it can be fine!" We all laugh and cram into the puny Pajero, sitting on one another's laps with our bags hanging out the windows but our spirits lifted. It turns out that this is how many Africans travel every day, with up to twenty people crammed into a tiny minivan. Thanks to Justus's positive thinking, the Pajero becomes part of our adventure, more of a funny joke than a failure. Between Justus and the Pajero, we will get many laughs over the next five weeks. And we will need them.

Our first time out on the streets of Nairobi, we are overwhelmed by the bustle and traffic all around. It's busier than any city I've seen in the U.S. There are many handmade wooden tables on the sidewalks where people sell all kinds of goods. Lots of these tables in one place make up the market, where local people buy their groceries, clothes, and hardware. The market is the perfect place to get the things we need for our quest all at once, but we soon realize that we don't know how to shop here! We look for bananas and discover that there are fifteen different types, some small and red, others orange, and still others big and green with a tough shell. Which table should we go to? Which bananas should we buy?

Luckily Justus knows just what to do. So after we drop off our gear at a nearby hotel, we hit the market to shop. We visit at least four different tables just for our food—a vegetable table, a rice table, a fruit table, and a bread table. We visit a table that sells only toys, where we buy yo-yos and balloons to give to kids along the way. Finally, for the last items on our list, we go to a table that sells water jugs, candles, toilet paper, and other necessities.

I pass a table that has clothes piled all over it. I suddenly remember that I forgot to bring a skirt in case we need to look nice for any important meetings. I take a quick look through the piles of clothes and am suddenly transported back in time. All the clothes look like they're from the U.S. in the '70s, or even the '60s. I see tight ski jackets with flared collars, bell-bottom corduroy pants, and tie-dyed T-shirts. This stuff certainly doesn't look African. Then it dawns on me. Churches across the U.S. collect used clothes from people, and missionaries give them to villagers all over Africa. Well, somehow the clothes have made it from the villages to the city, where they're being sold. I guess the villagers need money more than they need clothes—or maybe they just don't like the look! At first I get excited at the possibility of seeing something I myself donated years ago. Then I realize how sad it is that they can't afford new clothes, so they don't get to pick the colors and styles they really want.

I finally find a plain black skirt for a dollar.

While I'm paying, my stomach growls, and I realize I haven't eaten all day and I am sooo hungry. When I tell Justus, his face lights up and he leads me to his favorite place. It's a ramshackle hut made of plywood with a single bulb hanging over a few tables and a kitchen in the back that serves soup. When the soup arrives, I see long, stringy, wormy-looking things in it.

"What is it?" I ask Justus.

"Corn, beans, and some kind of meat, could be beef," he says.

I eye it suspiciously, thinking, *Yeah, maybe beef* worms . . . , but I'm so hungry I take a cautious bite. Mmm! Whatever it is, it's good!

We load our purchases into the Pajero, and Justus drives us to our hotel for a good night of sleep. The next morning we wake up refreshed and eager to head out of the city. But first we have to figure out how to get all our gear onto the Pajero. Justus takes a couple of the team members to find an auto shop that can build a rack. The rest of us stay behind and wait for hours and hours, wondering what could have happened to them. Finally, six hours later, they return looking tired and frustrated. But the little Pajero looks great with a brand-new, jet black rack on the roof. We hurry to load all the bags on top, tying them down securely. When we are done, we step back to admire our work and realize that all of us have black stripes over our clothes and hands. We try to brush them off and find that we are covered with sticky black tar, the "paint" that was used to make the rusty old metal rack look new! Once again we laugh and say, "It can be fine!" We're bound to get dirty anyway, right?

Finally, looking like a top-heavy donkey, the Pajero is ready to go. We look dubiously at the huge load, wondering if the SUV will tip right over. But we don't have time to waste, and we are dying to get out on the open road on our bikes and stretch our legs after the long preparations. We pack our panniers, which are like saddlebags that fit on the back of the bike, with what we'll need for the day, including food, water, and raincoats. The rest of the gear stays strapped atop the Pajero. We strap the panniers to our bike racks, put on our helmets, and double-check the maps. Just before we set off, Justus says he is worried. He urges us not to ride our bikes on the main roads. We look at one another, doubting his fears. Justus has already told us that he has never even ridden a bike, so we convince him that we know what we are doing and that we will be very careful.

We roll away from the hotel on our bikes and are immediately in heavy traffic, coughing and choking on car, bus, and truck fumes. Cars honk as they fly by, barely missing us. Once out of the heavy traffic, we breathe sighs of relief and some cleaner air. But then traffic slows again. I catch up to my eight teammates as they pull over. There is a traffic jam ahead, and we strain to see the cause. We get closer and join a group of school kids beside the road.

There's an old bicycle, smashed to pieces. Then we see that the kids are gathered around an African man on the ground. He isn't moving. I look away, tears welling up in my eyes. Nobody speaks; we just load our bikes and gear onto the Pajero and get in. From then on we never doubt Justus's judgment. He knows better than we do about the hazards of biking in Africa. Many roads don't have shoulders for bikers to ride along, and drivers don't make room for bikers. It is a sobering start to the trip, and we ride in silence, each of us wondering what lies ahead. . . .

For the next few hours, I strain my eyes looking out the window, searching for a savanna, a grassy plain dotted with acacia trees, where I might see a rhino or Cape buffalo, but all I see is village after village and people everywhere. Women walk along the road wearing multicolored cloths and carrying baskets balanced on their heads. It looks so graceful and leaves their hands free to carry their babies or packages. I even see one woman coming from the market with a basket full of live chickens on her head! The chickens look around like they are enjoying the ride. I make a mental note to try it myself when I get home. Well, maybe not with chickens.

Amid the brown village houses and dirt clearings we pass, something black and white catches my eye and I do a double take. Standing right next to the road is a real live African zebra—my first wild animal sighting! I'm so excited that I ask Justus to stop the car. As the zebra calmly walks across the road in front of us, I shoot half a roll of film. I hear car horns honking and realize that cars are backed up behind us and the local drivers are annoyed at us for stopping. I feel embarrassed, suddenly aware that they see me as a typical tourist.

Later I feel even sillier for making a big deal of a single zebra, because up ahead there are zebras everywhere, so many I can't count them. It turns out that Plains zebras are one of East Africa's most common wild animals. Many Africans consider them pests because zebras eat vegetables from peoples' gardens and compete with their livestock for the savanna grass.

Pests or no, the greatest sighting of the day is a big group of zebras, with a stallion, lots of mares, and nursing foals and fillies. I want to get out of the car to get a close-up shot, but Justus warns me to keep my distance. "Zebras can be fierce," he says. "They surround the babies and will kick you if they think you're a threat."

Later, with his eyes on the road, Justus tells me a myth about zebras that he learned as a child. Zebras, the story goes, were once donkeys. They worked so hard carrying heavy loads in the hot sun that their hooves were cracked and painful. One day a group of them got together and complained, "We work so hard. We should be running free like the gazelles." They went to see a man who was known to help animals in need. The man had some magic paint and offered to paint them so they wouldn't be recognized as donkeys. A few of the bravest donkeys stepped forward and received beautiful black-and-white-striped coats. They started prancing around, showing off. The rest, impatient to get their stripes, rushed forward in a stampede, breaking the paint pot and spilling all of the magic paint. The magic paint gone, the donkeys with stripes went racing off to become zebras and run free, while the donkeys without stripes were left behind to continue working for people.

As we drive on, Justus tells us stories about growing up in a Turkana village. The Turkana people are nomadic goat and cattle herders. They set up camps wherever the grazing is good and mainly live off the milk and blood of their animals. When Justus was only five or six years old, his father put him in charge of a small herd of goats, warning that if he lost a single animal in the desert, he would answer for it. Young Justus watched the goats anxiously, following them around, counting and recounting them and keeping them together by hitting the wanderers on the rear with a short stick.

One day he suddenly realized that he had lost a goat. He was terrified that the lost animal would be eaten by a hyena or a jackal. Since there was no one else to stay with the herd, he couldn't go looking for it. He could only run a short distance away to ask other herders if they'd seen his goat. Then he'd run back to his family's goats before another one could disappear. He searched all day long, but by nightfall he still had not found the missing goat. Frightened of what his father would do, Justus decided to stay out in the desert with the herd. After midnight his father found him and was angry at first. Then he realized that his harsh words kept Justus from returning safely home, and forgave him. The next day the goat was found, mixed in with another herd. Justus ends the story with a faraway look, then turns to us, laughs, and says, "After that, everything was fine."

Looking out at the endless towns, people, and shops lining the road out of the city, I marvel at the difference between Justus's childhood and my own. While I was listening to records and playing with toy horses and stuffed animals in my bedroom, Justus had real-life responsibilities and worries. I hope to learn more about Justus's way of life when we visit a Turkana village near Kenya's famous

26

Turkana Desert. I can hardly wait to get there, picturing all the animals I'll finally see in those open spaces.

My excitement builds as towns and people gradually give way to agricultural fields and we can get back on our bikes. Pedaling along, I can feel the ground becoming sandy and the fields turning into wide-open desert. But even when sand stretches to the horizon, the only animals I see are domestic goats, a few cows, and an occasional camel. Camels? I didn't expect to see camels in East Africa. They look so exotic next to the goats and cows. I wonder why people here keep camels. As for plants, there are very few, just scrubby round bushes that blow in the wind like tumbleweeds.

Ahead in the distance, there's a group of different plants, really big round bushes. Before I can identify these interesting new plants, dozens of children come pouring out of them, running to meet us! At first I'm confused, but Justus calls to us from the Pajero that these are the Turkana people. What I thought were big "bushes" are actually their houses! As we roll into the village, children gather all around us, fascinated by our bikes and helmets. Justus parks the Pajero and starts speaking to them in a language I've never heard.

One boy walks right up and introduces himself in broken English. "My name, Ekomwa." Just like the Turkana men, the boy carries a stick for herding livestock and is dressed in a light wool shawl and sandals made from recycled rubber truck tires. The shawl and sandals are traditional dress for the Turkana, but these days, instead of making their own cloth, they get the fabric from a local market. They make sandals out of tire rubber because it lasts longer than the leather they used to use. Many of the Turkana children speak a little English, taught to them by missionaries who come to start schools and health clinics in the villages.

Ekomwa invites me to his house, so I leave my bike for the other kids to play with and follow him. Like the other houses, Ekomwa's is made of sticks and mud, the only building materials in the area. Ekomwa pulls aside the cloth that covers the doorway and beckons me inside. Sitting on the dirt floor nursing a baby is a beautiful young woman, Ekomwa's mother. She is wearing dozens of blue beaded necklaces, bracelets, and earrings. Her head is shaved except for a strip of little beaded braids that stand straight up. Another small child, Ekomwa's brother Ekuwom, sits at her feet. I sit down and look around.

Everything inside is striped from the sunlight streaming through the cracks. For the

first time since arriving in Africa, I feel calm and protected. I can see out through the cracks, but the crowds outside can't see me. I feel like I am hiding inside a real bush, or in one of the cardboard forts I made as a kid. Sleepiness washes over me and I have the urge to take a little nap in this safe haven.

There is no furniture in the house, just a small depression in the dirt for a fire and a couple of gourd bowls hanging from the sticks in the wall. Turkana people don't cook much, since they live mainly on the blood and milk of their goats and cows. Ekomwa says, "Blood is gooood, tastes like liquid meat." He says blood is his favorite food, but he tried some cookies once and he liked them very much. Emerging from the house, Ekomwa shows me his playhouse, a tiny stick house he made that's exactly like his parents' house, with a cloth over the door and everything.

Though I would love to stay and play with Ekomwa and his little house, I hear my name called and am reminded of my mission. Reluctantly I say good-bye to Ekomwa and his family and return to the team.

Justus has arranged for me to talk to the village leader, Chief Tioko, and he is waiting for me.

Chief Tioko is dressed in a shawl like other Turkana men, but he also wears a nice velvet hat, which seems out of place in this remote location, where even basic necessities are not easy to come by. I remember the tables full of used clothes at the market in Nairobi and wonder if this was one of the missionaries' donated items. Maybe the chief liked the hat and chose to keep it rather than send it to market. The regal velvet certainly is fitting for his rank as chief. In addition to his smooth, well-worn herding stick, Chief Tioko carries an eksholong, a tiny, hand-carved wooden stool that doubles as chair and pillow, the Turkana man's only furniture for long herding trips. His stool is beautiful, made of one piece of wood, smoothed by use, and fitted with a handle made of soft braided leather. While I'm admiring the seat, he motions for me to try it out. Carefully I squat down on the tiny seat and it slides out from under me. Some kids nearby laugh out loud. Embarrassed, I try again and find that once I get the hang of it, the wooden seat is actually quite comfortable.

Justus translates while we talk. I ask Chief Tioko why there are no wild animals around us. "Ten years ago," he tells me, "this was lush green grassland. Many elephants, gazelles, and lions roamed here. But a very long drought turned the land to desert and drove them away. My people will rejoice when they return." I wonder why the land here changed. Perhaps the drought is a result of global warming. Or maybe there are too many people and grazing animals like goats eating up the plants and using all the water. Over many years, this could be turning the grasslands into desert.

When I say good-bye to Chief Tioko, I give him a small amount of money in appreciation for the time he spent with me. To my surprise, he gives me his little stool! I try to give him more money, thinking the stool must have taken a long time to make, but he waves it away, saying it's a gift, something to remember this day. I'm touched and promise him that I will carry it with me on the back of my bike wherever I go.

# 3. Lost

After leaving Chief Tioko, I decide to take a walk into the desert behind the Turkana village. I am deep in thought about the area's drought, and suddenly I realize I'm no longer on the trail. I am lost and alone in the desert in 115-degree heat and nearly out of water. I look in every direction and see only sand and bushes. I walk this way and that, getting more panicked, hot, and thirsty. Trying to get a grip on myself, I sit in the shade of a straggly bush. I'm sitting there just a few minutes when my thoughts are interrupted by a twitchy feeling on my leg. I look down and am surprised to find my legs covered with dark spots of dirt. Then I realize there is no dirt, only miles and miles of sand. Not only that, but the dark spots are moving. . . . Ewww, *ticks*! I grab one off my leg and throw it down on the sand. Like a tiny, indestructible, heat-seeking missile, it hops right up and heads straight for me again.

Totally disgusted, I rush from the bush back out into the hot sun, sit down, and remove all the ticks I can see. I am sitting wondering how I will find my way back when another motion catches my attention. It's a perfect ball, rolling all by itself across the sand. I pick it up to see what's underneath, but there's nothing on the ground. Carefully inspecting the ball, I find a large, shiny, green insect dangling underneath. A dung beetle! I put it back on the ground and immediately the ball starts to roll again, seemingly all by itself. I lie down on the ground and look underneath. The beetle is upside-down, pushing the ball with its back legs and walking backward on its front legs. It looks like a circus acrobat, rolling the ball while doing a handstand!

Dung beetles, as their name suggests, love dung (the proper name for poop). They are born in dung, spend their lives searching for dung, and probably die in dung, too. Gross? Not if you're a dung beetle. I follow the beetle's swerving path through the sand back to a huge pile of fibrous dung, unmistakably elephant. *So there* are *elephants here,* I think, looking around with new hope.

It might seem strange, but animal poop is very valuable, not only to dung beetles, but also to wildlife biologists. When scientists are trying to study a rare or shy animal, the animal's dung may be the only evidence they can find. The contents of the dung can tell you what an animal has been eating. The size of the dung can tell you whether the animal is large or small. A scientist can tell whether an animal is healthy or sickly from the contents and consistency of its dung and also get an idea of the number of animals in a particular area from the amount of dung there.

Weighing about ten pounds and full of sticks, the dung I have discovered could come from none but the largest land mammal. I can tell from the dung that the elephant has been eating grass and bushes, complete with the branches. It looks like a big, round loaf of super-healthy whole wheat bread. It's dry on the outside, not very fresh. Picking it apart with a stick, I find more dung beetles inside, busy rolling the soft inner dung into balls. Making dung balls is serious business for male dung beetles, since female dung beetles may choose their mate by the size and craftsmanship of his dung ball.

I look around again hopefully for some elephants but see only sand and scraggly bushes, and no trail anywhere in sight. I'm frustrated to find a sign of elephants but not see them. I guess elephants can travel a long way in a day, and this dung may be a few days old.

**W**ell, thinking about the elephants and dung beetles took my mind off the ticks, but I've still got to find my way back to the village and some water. I search and search, squinting my eyes and trying to think like a goat or camel. Finally, I find a tiny goat path, barely visible, winding through the sand and thorns. It takes me straight to the village.

I arrive at the group of huts relieved, but desperately in need of water. I scan the village and find a bike bottle one of my teammates must have left behind. After a long drink, I go looking for Justus. He's on the other side of the village, in the middle of a group of women. Some are old and some are young, but all wear thick layers of beaded necklaces and large hoops in their stretched-out earlobes. They are all yelling.

When I walk up to Justus, a couple of girls say something to him and point at me. One is tall and lovely and wears so many necklaces, they seem to make her neck even longer. She looks at me with piercing eyes and just stares, like she's angry with me. I look at the ground.

"What's going on?" I quietly ask Justus.

"They want to jump with you," he says, as if it's the most normal thing in the world. "They say if you don't come back in the morning they'll kidnap you." With that, both girls give me a mischievous look, laugh, and duck into one of the round stick huts. A little confused, I follow Justus out of the village and go help the team set up camp. My mind is racing as we put up the tents. What does it mean, that they want to jump with me? Are they serious about kidnapping me? That night I am so nervous and excited I can barely sleep.

In the morning, we emerge from our tents

and walk over to the village. When we arrive, forty or fifty people greet us with songs. All the women, young and old, join hands, form a circle, and begin an eerie, high, trilling scream. It reminds me of a battle cry and makes my hair stand on end. Then they start a slow, rhythmic, jumping dance and begin to sing. Before I know it, the two girls grab me and I am swept into the circle. They take my sunglasses and give me a large necklace, like a flat, round collar of vibrant blue, orange, and white beads. The traditional necklace looks funny with my T-shirt and shorts, but one of the girls looks funny, too, wearing my glasses upside down with her traditional clothes. Many of the women are bare-breasted and wear an amazing array of patterned cloths, called kangas, wrapped around their slender waists. The older women wear so many necklaces that you can't see their necks. Necklaces are a sign of status and age. Little girls start out with one necklace and get more as they grow older.

The women are jumping all around me,

laughing and holding my hands. They try to teach me the words of the song, something like "A lo loma, a ya ya lo loma." Just when I think I'm getting the hang of it, they laugh at me and I know that what I'm saying sounds silly to them. We keep jumping and jumping, sometimes up and down all together and

sometimes in pairs, one going up while the other goes down, like a seesaw. When I get tired and try to pull away, they just laugh and change the song, but hold onto my hands and keep on jumping, jumping, jumping. I am exhausted, but whirling in a happy, dizzy daze. After a while, I get lost in the movement and the words of the song. I feel relaxed and free, like I could go on jumping forever. When the singing finally stops, I don't even know how long I've been dancing.

When it comes time to leave the village, we are offered a special treat . . . a wooden bowl full of fresh, bright red goat's blood! When the bowl comes to me, I look at it and smile, trying not to be rude. I turn to Justus for help, but he just nods encouragingly. Of course, he's Turkana, too, so he loves to drink fresh blood. Luckily, the girls take the bowl away and offer it to Justus instead. He drinks the whole thing in one gulp and looks up with a big, red-rimmed smile. It looks just like a milk mustache, only red. It occurs to me that bleeding livestock is not really that different from milking them, since the Turkana take just a little blood at a time and say that it doesn't hurt the animals much. I ask Justus later what blood tastes like and he says, "Blood is so good; it tastes just like liquid meat." After hearing the same testimonial from Ekomwa and Justus, I think there must be something to it and decide to try goat's blood the next time it is offered.

As I turn to go, I notice a man in the distance, sitting in front of his hut on a tiny stool just like mine. I look fondly over at my bike, with the little stool strapped on the back, and feel a connection to the people who live here. After visiting Ekomwa's home, talking to Chief Tioko, and dancing with the Turkana girls, I have a much better sense of what Turkana life is like. I leave the village with a warm feeling, amazed that people with so little of what I thought was necessary are so generous and seem so happy.

# 4. Tenting in Hippo Territory

Still determined to find animals, we decide to look for hippos at Lake Baringo in central Kenya. We arrive late at night and hurry to make camp, since it's already dark and mosquitoes are swarming all around us. I look for a good camp spot, but since it's pitch dark, I can't tell one spot from another and just walk out into an open space and set up my tent. I go back to the Pajero to fill my water bottle, then finally, around 1:00 A.M., say good-night to Justus, and stumble back toward my tent for a good night's sleep. I need a rest for the busy day of hippo hunting ahead.

On the way to my tent, a big, dark shape startles me. I shine my light and see a huge shadow glide past, smooth and gray like a blimp. Could it be . . . *a hippo?* I stop short, barely daring to breathe, listening and waiting. Mosquitoes buzz in my ears and stab through my clothes. I struggle to stay still and quiet, but the mosquitoes make me want to jump up and down and scream. Finally, when I think the hippo isn't looking, I slip into my tent. *CRACK! CRUNCH! SNORT! MUNCH!* The noise of hippos belching and rumbling, breaking sticks with their heavy, thudding feet, surrounds my tent. It sounds like there is an army of hippos right outside.

I've heard that hippos are the most dangerous animals in Africa, killing more people each year than lions, elephants, or Cape buffalo. People are often killed by mistake when a hippo is startled and runs toward the water, trampling whatever's in its way. I definitely do *not* want to startle a hippo and end up looking like a pancake. I lie still in my sleeping bag, listening and waiting, paralyzed with fear. The rest of the night is a tense, half-awake blur. I hear hippos crunching and munching and imagine them shoving their way through my tent door, staring at me with their beady eyes and big teeth.

When I awaken, I discover I have unwittingly camped right near the lakeshore. All around my tent is evidence of the hippo party from the night before: footprints the size of dinner plates, broken sticks, and splattered

dung. In the light of day I see for the first time the signs all around camp that say WATCH OUT FOR HIPPOS, WILD ANIMALS ARE DANGEROUS, and DO NOT PROCEED PAST THIS SIGN AFTER 7:00 P.M. Then I learn that a man lost his leg to a hippo only two weeks before, right near my tent.

In spite of being a little shaken up, I am thrilled that I got so close to hippos and lived to tell about it. After I move my tent to a safer spot away from the lakeshore, we go into a nearby village and ask around to find someone with a motorboat, so we can go searching for hippos in the lake. Surprisingly, the narrow boat we rent holds ten people. It feels tipsy, though. This makes us all nervous: Many hippo-related deaths happen when a hippo capsizes a boat and drowns or bites the people who fall out. We cautiously make our way, looking for a swampy area of tall grasses, perfect hippo habitat.

We putter along close to shore because we know hippos much prefer walking and bounding along the bottom in shallow water to swimming in deep water. We arrive at a swampy area and look around for telltale hippo ears and eyes sticking up above water. Baby hippos are the easiest to spot, since they have to rise up to breathe about every thirty seconds, while adult hippos can stay hidden underwater for up to fifteen minutes.

Soon after we arrive, a baby hippo emerges from below like a submarine. It breaks the surface with a loud breath: *Shew!* We stop the engine so we don't scare it. Even the baby seems huge to me—its head is two feet long. Still, it looks like a baby, with its big, sur-

prised eyes. What is it like to be a baby hippo, riding on Mom's back and playing in the water all day long?

Right behind the baby, a mama hippo breaks the surface with an even louder breath: *SHEEEEW!* Talk about huge—she makes the baby look tiny! We start the engine and back up, knowing that mama hippos protecting their babies can be deadly. More hippos surface, one after another, out of breath and unable to stay hidden from us any longer. As soon as they get a breath, they go back under, and the water around us ripples with hippos bobbing up and down. There must be thirty hippos right around our boat! When most of the hippos are underwater again, we look at one another nervously, wondering exactly where all those hippos are. I hope one isn't under the boat!

After another close encounter with hippos, you'd think I would have gotten enough of them for one day, but walking back to camp, I find myself hatching a plan. Tonight, instead of being scared by hippo noises, I am determined to spot a hippo out of the water.

I rush through dinner, anxious to get back to my tent to prepare for the hippos' arrival. I put brand-new batteries in my headlamp and flashlight. I put new batteries in my camera, too, because without a photo, I know no one will believe me. Finally, I'm dressed and ready to go. I sit on my sleeping bag in the dark, armed with two lights and a camera, and wait. After a while I start to doze.

A loud *CRACK!* right outside the tent makes me spring up, wide awake. Then I tiptoe around inside my tent, stopping to determine the direction of the noise. I think the hippo making the noise has stopped, too, and is probably standing on the other side of the tent fabric, stock-still just like I am. I take a deep breath, get close to the window, then flip on my headlamp, expecting a huge hippo to burst into view. I sweep my head to the right, then to the left. No hippo. How could a three-ton blimp hide in a grassy clearing?

I shouldn't go out-side, but my curiosity gets the better of me. I unzip the door and step into the night. It is eerily quiet; not even a mosquito is buzzing.

I imagine hundreds of animals watching me from the trees as I step around the corner of my tent and flip on my light, expecting a huge hippo. Nothing. I creep around the next corner, see a movement, and flip on my light again.

Surprise! I stop in my tracks, stunned at what I see.

In front of me is a tall, thin African man holding a huge, sharp spear. In the dark he looks like a warrior. We stare at each other in what I think is a standoff. My pulse is racing and I'm plotting my escape. Then he says, "I'm the night watchman. Do you need some-thing?" I pause, dumbfounded, then say,

"Have you . . . seen any hippos tonight?" "Oh, no," he says, laughing. "You are completely safe. I have already chased all the hippos away for the night." I'm disappointed about my failed hippo ambush but realize how funny the whole situation is. This man is hired to keep hippos away from tourists, and here I am trying to run into one in the dark! I secretly wish I could be the one to chase the hippos away each night.

The next morning it's time to head off again, toward Samburu National Park. As we bike away from the lake, the land gets drier, but with bigger bushes and clumps of trees. The road to Samburu is long and dusty, and by afternoon we are all dirty and tired. As we arrive at the park entrance, we come upon a group of the most striking, elaborately dressed women I've ever seen. They are wearing bright red wrap skirts, with loads of jewelry and incredible hairdos. Looking at myself in my sweaty, dirt-brown clothes, I feel even

grubbier, and wonder how they can stay so clean and fresh looking in the dusty environment. Some have long braids while others have their hair packed in red mud paste with beads woven in. Some even have beaded visors attached to their hair and fake flowers sprouting up like little fountains from the tops of their heads. Only one thing is odd. They all have rippling muscles and are leaning against huge spears.

Then it dawns on me that these are not women but tall, thin, muscular men! When I look back at their skirts and hairdos, I can't help but stare. Justus gives me a stern look, informing me that these are the Morani, elite warriors of the Samburu tribe, and I must be very respectful. As teenagers, they are initiated into adulthood in a ceremony that, until recently, involved killing a lion. After that they are banished from the village for five years to fend for themselves, finding and killing their food in the bush. Once they are fully trained, they are responsible for protecting the village and its cattle.

I am very curious about the warriors and want to ask a few questions, but when I approach, the men ignore me, acting busy tending to one another's hair and beads. I try not to take it personally and wonder if I'm breaking some traditional Samburu code of behavior. When one glares right at me, I decide to learn what I can about the Samburu from Justus instead.

We walk along a small dirt track to the village and he tells me about their culture. He says that as wild animal populations decline, the Samburu people's practices are changing. They rarely kill lions anymore. In fact, these days they actively help protect lions and other wildlife in the park, especially elephants.

We pass a woman with a little baby, and Justus points out the baby's necklace, which has a small white bead in the middle. He tells me that it's a charm made of elephant bone to protect the baby for its entire life. When a young Samburu couple marries, a pile of elephant dung is burned on the floor of their house to bless them with a long and happy life together.

An old Samburu story says that long, long ago, people and elephants worked together as friends. The women of the village would ask elephants to bring firewood to their houses. One day an elephant brought a few of the nicest branches he could find, but one of the women yelled at him, "This is barely enough to keep a mouse warm!" The next time the elephant came back dragging several large trees, roots and all, but now one of the women complained, "They're far too large to be of any use!" Then the elephant got mad. In a rage he swept through the village, pushing over trees and destroying houses. He kept some of the cowhide shingles he had ripped off the houses and made them into the floppy ears you still see on elephants today. He decided to go into the wild where the women couldn't yell at him, but before he left he said, "When we meet again, we will be enemies." Since that day elephants have been wild and people have come to fear, respect, and admire them. But people and elephants will never again live together as they did many years ago.

Justus finishes the story just as we see a Samburu man wearing camouflage clothing instead of a skirt and carrying a big rifle instead of a spear. Justus says he is a guard, trying to protect the elephants in the park from their biggest enemy, poachers, illegal hunters who shoot elephants for their ivory tusks. I learn that in 1988 poachers killed an average of three elephants a day in Kenya alone. Kenya's elephant population dropped from about 140,000 to only about 15,000 in the '80s. Today poaching is on the rise again, so the Samburu patrol the park, looking for illegal hunters. The Samburu also act as expert guides, teaching tourists to appreciate the beauty of the animals they know and love.

Later in the day, when we visit the Samburu school, dozens of children come out clapping and singing. In clear, high-pitched voices, they call out a beautiful song that describes the elephant's noble character. As the chorus repeats "Oh, Mr. Elephant, your ears are mighty large," a tiny elephant comes walking out of the schoolhouse. The elephant acts so real, shuffling its feet and swinging its trunk, that it takes me a minute to realize it is two children inside an elaborate costume made of burlap sacks. They put on a terrific show.

**R**iding slowly through Samburu Park in the Pajero, we are stopped dead in our tracks by a ruckus of bellowing, screeching, and splashing just around the corner. I look at Justus for some clue about what danger might lie ahead, but he looks unconcerned. As we come around a clump of trees, we find a whole group of elephants bathing and playing by a river!

I'm spellbound, watching two teenage males face off on top of a dirt mound, which Justus tells me is a termite nest. They lock tusks, wrapping their trunks around each other in a playful tug-of-war.

Nearby a baby elephant clumsily fiddles around by the riverside, learning to suck water into its trunk to drink and bathe. Excited, I move too quickly and bang my camera against the window. The big Mama elephant shakes her head and flaps her ears, scolding me. I cower, wondering if she might charge us, but she is distracted just in time by a big splash in the water nearby.

In the next instant, a big crocodile slides up onto the riverbank right near the baby elephant. Mama stomps her feet and flaps her ears and trots over to chase the croc back into the water. Even that big croc is scared of Mama elephant.

The baby takes a big trunk full of water from the river and showers himself with it. Then he flops down in the mud and rolls around. He looks like he is having such fun. . . .

A loud noise threatens, and we turn around to find Mama elephant right behind us, scolding. I can't believe that such a huge animal could move so silently. We are looking up at her towering over the SUV, wondering what to do, when she throws her trunk in the air and blasts us with a sound so loud we have to cover our ears. She stomps her feet and flaps her ears, once again scolding us for getting too close to her baby. At once she's gone. All the elephants have disappeared into the bush, and the riverbank is empty. I think Mama elephant told the rest of the herd to follow her, but how did they all understand and act so quickly? "Ah," I suddenly realize, big Mama elephant must be the oldest female and matriarch, or leader, of the group.

I remember reading about elephants' ability to communicate with vibration—super low, or infrasonic, sounds that people can't hear. I wonder if that's how she got the others to follow so quickly. As the matriarch, Mama elephant is the family group's most important member. Being the oldest, she's the one that remembers where water can be found in years of intense drought. And she probably remembers seeing huge crocodiles attack baby elephants. By chasing that croc, she was not only saving her baby, she was teaching the other females in the group to do the same.

Leaving the river, Justus stops by the side of the road and gets out to show us a pile of bones, really *big* bones. Next to the bones I notice large, round depressions in the dust. Elephant tracks. The bones look like they've been dragged around and piled together. Wow! I had heard that elephants recognize elephant bones and carcasses and often spend time examining them, picking them up, and sometimes even burying them, but I didn't expect to actually see an elephant graveyard!

Why do elephants show such interest in bones? To me, it's exciting to think that elephants understand death and are capable of deep emotions, much like humans. Some people, however, think that elephants are just so smart and curious that they are attracted to bones as kids are attracted to building blocks and other toys. Scientists aren't sure how much elephants understand about bones. It remains an amazing animal mystery for us to ponder.

Researcher Cynthia Moss studied and lived among one family of elephants for thirteen years. She says elephants don't pay much attention to other animal bones or carcasses, but they act strange when they come upon an elephant carcass.

One story particularly amazes me. Cynthia had come across a dead female and brought her jawbone to camp to determine the elephant's age. A few days later her family came into camp, went straight to the jawbone, and spent a long time inspecting it. One young elephant stayed long after the others had gone, repeatedly feeling and stroking the jaw and turning it with his foot and trunk. He was the dead elephant's seven-year-old son, her youngest calf. Cynthia felt sure that he recognized his mother.

Thinking about these large, intelligent animals, I look down near my foot and see a big, football-shaped elephant poop. I pick it up and hurl it into the bush with a whoop, hoping for a nice spiral. Instead it flies into a million pieces. Come and get it, dung beetles!

# 5. Camel Rides
# and Baboon Friends

We say good-bye to the kids, warriors, and elephants and drive on from Samburu Park. I am still thinking about them when we come upon a makeshift village constructed of tents and shacks. Next to one of the shacks is a group of camels. Still curious about camels in Africa, I ask Justus to pull over. As we walk closer to the camels, one of them fixes its huge brown eyes on me with a look of seeming disgust. Then the camel lets out a loud, whining scream, which makes me jump! A tall, thin man wearing loose cotton clothing stands up from where he was sitting next to the camels and says, "You want to ride the champion?" Only then do I notice that the very camel that screamed is wearing a saddle and has a simple bridle in its mouth. The man proudly explains that this camel won the prestigious village camel race here three years in a row. So the camels are for riding, like horses! I ask him if the camels are pets and he looks away as if he didn't hear me. I wonder if he knows what it means to have a pet. Ignoring my question, he asks me again if I want a ride, so I nod eagerly.

He grabs the champion camel by the bridle, pulling it to the ground. The camel complains loudly and shakes its head, splattering the man and me with a long line of foamy drool that hung from its lip. Blech!

I'm not so sure this camel wants to be ridden, so I motion for the man to stop. But he yanks again and the camel drops to its knees. Even when the camel is kneeling down, its huge hump is taller than I am. There is a tiny saddle perched on top of the hump. I'm nervous, but I think, *I've ridden a horse; I should be fine.* As if he can hear my thoughts, Justus says, "It can be fine."

Stepping up high, I get my feet into the stirrups, but even before I can get settled in the little saddle, the camel starts to stand. It straightens its front feet, and its body rises to a sharp angle. I'm thrown backward, then suddenly forward as the camel straightens its back feet. Feeling silly, I look down at Justus far below and then lurch forward again as the man hits the camel on the rear. The camel looks back at me with its big eye and frothy mouth and moves slowly forward, throwing me this way and that with each step. After just a few minutes, my back cramps up and my legs are sore. I plead to get off.

The man laughs and says, "No race?"

"No! No race, please!" As the camel kneels down, I'm prepared and manage the lurching motions a little more gracefully. Phew! Nearing the ground, I jump off gratefully and step away. As I look up at the camel, it looks down at me with what feels like a new gaze of superiority as if it has won and I have lost.

As I still wipe camel spit from my arm and rub my sore legs, we leave the man with the camels and look around the makeshift village. Most of the shacks are made of corrugated metal and are full of people. We peek in and see many beds and piles of clothing. A few shacks have tables out in front covered with jewelry for sale.

A young boy with high cheekbones comes out to try to sell us his bracelets, saying, "Look here, good price, good copper metal."

We look at his jewelry and compliment him on the attractive patterns of bright metals. We ask where he's from. "Ethiopia," he says. The people here are refugees from fighting in their country. When we ask him where he gets the nice copper, he points to an electrical pole near the village. I look down the power lines and see some of the wires hanging free. Farther down, an entire pole is pulled to the ground and lies hacked to pieces. I recognize the pieces of electrical pole in a wood fire in which some people are cooking meat. It's sad to realize that these people are so desperate that they've cut the lines to meet their immediate needs.

We buy a few bracelets from the Ethiopian boy and look for a market to buy some fresh food. Everyone we ask points to the same shack, so we head over to explore. Inside we find a few tables and a menu handwritten in Ethiopian. All of a sudden, I am so impressed by this resourcefulness and creativity. With just a few chairs set up in a shack, a handwritten sign, some hacked-up telephone poles to roast meat, and some copper wire, the Ethiopians have created an impromptu restaurant and beautiful jewelry to make money off tourists!

The menu features only three items, none of which I can pronounce. We use hand signals to order one of each dish and wait anxiously, wondering what we will get. When the food comes out, it is steaming hot. It looks like a mix of vegetables and meat in what smells like a curry sauce. We ask about the type of meat, but we can't understand the waiter and he can't understand us. We point at the meat and try to imitate a goat, making little ears with our fingers and little bleating goat noises. The waiter seems to understand us, but shakes his head no and pretends to be a larger animal. Hmm. We haven't seen any cows around here, but we taste the meat and decide it must be beef, just a little tougher than the beef we're used to.

We finish all the dishes and pay for the meal, feeling quite satisfied. The man is exceedingly happy with the money we have given him and he follows us out the door, shaking our hands and bowing repeatedly. As we turn to leave, he taps me on the shoulder and points in the distance, right at the man with the camels. I smile and make a motion like I am riding a camel. He nods and smiles and makes an eating motion. Agh! I start to feel sick, realizing I just ate camel meat.

**W**e have an appointment with some lion researchers in Laikipia, Kenya, and it's a whole day's drive to get there. Once again we find ourselves bumping along yet another dirt road. Just when I think I'm getting used to the

Pajero's cramped space and hard seats, we hit a pothole and I get a new bruise. At least the monotony of the dusty drive is broken when a herd of giraffes runs across the road right in front of us. Later we catch up to the giraffes along the road and watch them eat leaves from the top of a tall acacia, a thorny, scraggly tree common in East Africa.

I am just wondering how they can chew up the huge sharp thorns when one giraffe opens its mouth and sticks out a long, dark bluish, ultra-slimy, snakelike thing! The giraffe wraps this weird tongue around a branch and pulls it in, thorns and all. When the giraffe chews, long strings of slime stretch and snap back to its mouth. Justus tells me the slimy stuff is super-thick saliva around the tongue that coats the thorns and protects the giraffe's throat. What must it feel like to have a mouthful of gooey slime and sharp thorns? I guess it's the price giraffes pay in order to survive in the African wilderness. Who ever said natural selection was easy?

After a long night camped in a field and a bit more lurching along dirt roads in the morning, we finally arrive at a group of buildings with metal roofs—the scientific research station. Jason Hassrick and Brendan Bowles greet us at the door. Wearing rugged clothes and knives on their belts, they look more like happy adventurers than nerdy scientists. They offer us breakfast before we head out. As we wolf down eggs, toast, and coffee, they look on amazed. We have to explain that we've run out of food. Last night we ate the last of our supplies for dinner—stale cornflakes and kidney beans. We mixed them together and made the best of it, joking that it was just like chili and corn bread!

After breakfast I ask Jason what he and Brendan do. As he talks, I start to understand the complexity of their mission. "Basically, ranchers and wildlife haven't been getting along too well around here," he begins. Jason tells me that Africa's human population is growing too fast and the land can't keep up. To survive, people cut down trees to make gardens and raise cattle. Wild predators like hyenas and lions are either pushed out of the area or they learn to kill cattle. And when lions and hyenas kill cattle, they usually get shot. Jason feels for both the people and the wildlife, explaining that each is just trying to survive; but there's not enough room for everybody. It's easy to understand when you realize that there are about a million babies born each year in Kenya alone.

Jason explains that every time a predator like a lion is killed, another lion takes over its territory. The new lion might not have lived around people and learned to fear them, so each new lion that moves in attacks cattle and ends up getting shot. To avoid this, Jason and Brendan are trying to educate both the lions and the ranchers.

"And how do you educate lions, exactly?" I ask, looking at him skeptically. He tells me there are many ways to "teach" lions to be afraid of people.

Jason and Brendan have found that when ranchers leave dogs and fires around their cattle pens at night, predators learn to stay away, hunting wildlife instead of the easier-to-catch cattle. If lions don't attack, people won't shoot them. They also want ranchers to learn that wild animals are an important part of a healthy ecosystem. Jason and Brendan encourage the ranchers to take pride in the predators. Instead of shooting lions and hyenas, some ranchers are even starting to make extra money by guiding tourists around their land to see the wildlife.

When everyone's finally finished eating, we hit the road to see what Jason and Brendan do on a typical day. I'm standing up with my head out the window to relieve my sore butt when we suddenly hit a wall of stench that makes me gag. Jason stops his jeep. I'm thinking, *Can't we stop somewhere that doesn't stink?* But before I can complain, he is out of the jeep and going into the bushes, right toward the stench! We don't want to be left on the road alone with lions and hyenas around, so we follow him. A few feet into the bushes, we hear a low growl, then see a female spotted hyena in a big cage.

The source of the stench is all too clear now—a big chunk of rotten meat was used as bait. The trap has not harmed the animal, but there is a telltale trench encircling the cage with hyena claw marks and tracks all around, evidence that the hyena's sisters tried to dig her out in the night. Spotted hyena clans are led by females, and the bond between sisters is strong.

In the cage, too, there are scratches and a little blood from the hyena trying to dig her way out. I feel sad for her, but realize that the information we gather may help save hyenas in the end. The sooner we're done, the sooner she can go home. We all dive in to help Jason do a thorough physical examination.

First Jason darts her with a tranquilizer; then we wait for it to take effect. In just a few minutes, she lies down in the cage and falls fast asleep. We reach in and pull her out, then carry her over to a blue tarp on the grass. My job is to pick off ticks, look inside her mouth, and measure her long, razor-sharp canines. A heavy load of parasites like ticks might indicate a weak animal, while the size and wear of her teeth can tell us her age. Jason also checks her nipples and discovers that she is producing milk, which means she has young pups back at her den. The last step is to attach a radio collar around her neck. The radio collar looks like a large dog collar with a small box on the top. It will help scientists find out where the hyenas are living and hunting.

While I'm leaning close to her, searching for ticks, Jason says, "Smell the fur behind her ears and tell me what it smells like." Naturally curious, I smell behind her ears. I'm amazed; she smells like my dogs after a bath. Then, with my hand inside her mouth, measuring her teeth, she wakes and stands up! We all jump up in a panic and run helter-skelter, bumping into one another and lunging for cover. We look back to see her flop down again in the grass, unable to stand. Jason stifles a laugh, knowing it'll be another fifteen minutes before the tranquilizer wears off and she can actually walk again.

When we're finished, I take a last look at her. She looks small and defenseless lying there on the blue tarp with the new collar on. But, I realize, in just a short while she'll be running wild with her sisters again, an incredibly powerful and truly wild animal. She stirs again and we creep quietly back through the bushes to let her wake up in peace.

That afternoon we have to be on our way. Jason and Brendan say good-bye and give us directions to a town where we can restock our supplies, laughing again about the morning's eating frenzy.

I've learned a lot about hyenas from Jason and Brendan and I've decided that hyenas have a bad rap. I always heard they were vicious, stinky, rotten, meat-eating scavengers that stole kills from lions. Well, among all the other things I learned about hyenas, I found out that they hunt most of their food themselves and many of their kills are actually stolen by lions. When I go home, I'm going to teach everybody the truth about hyenas!

Our next visit is nearby with researcher Shirley Strum, who has been coming to Kenya for thirty years to study friendship among one of our closest relatives, baboons. I can't wait to see baboons up close and personal.

Shirley's headquarters is a house made of

logs and stone set in the middle of a five-thousand-acre ranch in the shadow of Mount Kenya. Hearing us drive up, she steps out and calls, "You made it! It's almost dusk, so go ahead and set up your tents. . . . Just watch out for snakes."

The moon is full, and I'm eager to camp out on the open savanna. I fall asleep listening to the pleasant sounds of insects, but about an hour later, I wake up to noises that make my hair stand on end. Hearing a sudden burst of bloodcurdling screams and low, growling roars that can't be more than thirty feet from my tent, I don't know what to do. When they stop, I whisper to Justus in the next tent, "Did you hear that?"

"Yes," he replies, in a hoarse whisper, "lions."

I sit awhile, silent and motionless, then whisper again, "What should we do?" There's no response. *He must really be scared*, I think. Then after a minute or two, a loud snore comes from his tent.

In the morning Shirley smiles slightly when I tell her about almost becoming a lion snack. She says, "I heard them, too. They're actually cubs—and they were pretty far away. If they were grown lions and really close, you'd have to cover your ears and your insides would vibrate." When I find out I wasn't actually in danger, I'm embarrassed about being so scared. But more than that, I wish I had seen the cubs; they must have been adorable, growling and snarling like that! I feel closer to my dream of seeing lions in the wild, but still frustrated at not actually seeing them. Well, at least hearing cubs is a start.

Shirley takes us to see the baboons she's been studying, a group of thirty or so she calls the Pumphouse Gang. She takes us to their sleeping spot, and when they wake up and begin feeding, she introduces us to some of her favorites—a big male named Ram and two females, Rebecca and Elka. As Rebecca's new baby nurses, he looks up at his mother and twirls her hair in the fingers of his free hand. I can't stop staring, amazed at how human the mother and baby look. Ram patiently lets his friend, a little baby named Eric, climb right up his face and pinch his nose, behavior that nor-mally wouldn't be toler-ated. "Baboons make friends with other baboons," Shirley says. "Just like humans, everyone needs friends to survive."

As the baboons forage, they pick up, examine, and eat just about everything they come across, from grasses and flowers to termites and caterpillars. They even dissect other animals' poop to find the tasty undigested seeds inside. Shirley tells us they eat more than a hundred different types of food.

A young baboon named Ralph looks mischievously at me and reaches out to grab my pant leg as I walk by. I want to play with him, but Shirley warns me not to touch or even look at him. She says he is trying to intimidate me, and if I respond, it will mean I want to pick a fight. I keep my hands to myself, but my curiosity gets the better of me and I sneak just one peek at the cute little guy. The eye contact is enough to threaten him and he runs right at me, shrieking. Luckily, it's just a bluff, and at the last second he dodges me and runs past to pick on a smaller baboon instead. Shrieks and snarls come up from behind a rock as they tussle. Oops!

# 6. Meeting the Hadza Tribe

We have to leave Shirley and the baboons, because today we are going to drive across the Kenyan border into Tanzania. Then we'll be biking in search of a small group of people called the Hadza, the last true hunter-gatherers of East Africa. Even fifty years ago, there were still many tribes all over East Africa who lived in temporary camps, hunting wildlife and gathering roots and other things to eat. But in today's more modern world, with its wildlife parks and fenced cattle ranches, that way of life is rapidly disappearing. I can't help but think the decline in wildlife and the decline in people like the Hadza are linked. I'm eager to see this tribe and find what clues I can.

As we near the Kenya/Tanzania border, the land turns into grassy, rolling hills dotted with acacias. We drive past a sign for Maasai Mara National Reserve. We have been riding for six hours, and our legs are stiff. "Can't we get out and take a hike?" I plead to Justus.

"When we get to the edge of the park, we will stop," he assures me. When we arrive at the main park gates, Justus talks to the guard. We can't understand what they are saying, but we get the feeling they are friends. The guard seems to be giving Justus directions, and then they say good-bye with lots of handshakes and patting of each other's arms.

Inside the park the land seems wilder. The Mara River runs through the grassy hills, and all around there are lots and lots of ter-mite mounds, and each one seems to have an animal on top! I remember the elephants wrestling on the termite mound and ask

Justus about it. He doesn't know about the elephants but says these antelopes, called topis, are territorial males that stand on top of termite mounds in order to scout for other males or predators. The topis are silly looking to me. They have purplish black patches covering their face, shoulders, and rump, and they look like they are wearing white stockings.

I'm scanning the horizon for more topis when I see a different, much lower, slinky-looking shape on top of a mound. We get closer, and I see spots! As the rumbling Pajero approaches, the cheetah struts gracefully down the mound. The animal is so thin, it reminds me of a greyhound. Like a shadow, the cheetah walks away from the road, and in an instant it is gone.

We drive off the main dirt road onto a smaller track and stop at the bottom of a gently sloping hill.

"What are we doing?" I ask Justus.

"You want to hike, yes?" he asks, smiling.

We are confused because we didn't think hiking inside the park was allowed, but we follow Justus, not knowing if we will be gone for a few minutes or a few hours. He leads us up the hill until we see four men ahead, sitting next to the trail. They are dressed in military camouflage, and each one carries a semiautomatic rifle. Now we are really confused. Justus talks to the men, and one of them gets up. Like many men in this part of Africa, he is tall and thin. Justus tells us to go with him. We are starting to wonder what's going on here, but Justus waves us on. We trust him, so we follow the man. The man speaks no English, but he too keeps waving us on; come quickly, he seems to say.

Around a bend in the trail only about thirty feet from us, a big bush is rustling. Before we can say anything, an enormous rhino comes rumbling out! It sees us and looks startled, as if wondering what to do. I remember a program I saw on TV about vicious rhino attacks. We start to walk backward, tripping in our haste. But the man with the gun is calm, standing right in front of the rhino. *Now I understand why he has that huge rifle,* I think. The man turns and waves us toward him, toward the rhino. My mind asks, *Are you crazy?* but my mouth says, "Is it okay?"

He says, "Yes, okay, okay."

We look at one another and carefully move forward, keeping the man and his gun in between the rhino and us.

Suddenly, the rhino turns and lunges toward me. Panicked, I leap backward and catch my

foot on a root and fall right into a prickly little thorn bush. Ouch! I look up and catch the man with a smile on his face. Again he says, "Okay, okay," and walks toward the rhino. *Wow, he really isn't afraid,* I realize, walking right up behind him to take some photos. I'm thinking, *My mom is never going to believe this.* The rhino is within arms' reach. As it walks by, I see its dark little eyes and thick hide with big scratch marks, probably from rubbing against tree branches. I wonder whether it gets hot and itchy in that thick skin. We follow the rhino for a few minutes before it turns, rustles some branches, and disappears into a big bush.

We head down the hill, still amazed that we saw a rhino in the wild, and so close. When we get back to the Pajero, Justus is all smiles. That's when we know we've been had. Justus tells us, grinning, that the rhino was brought here as a baby to keep him safe from poachers and that those four men have been guarding him for the last five years. They patrol the park, but their main job is to stay close to the rhino, following him wherever he goes. Well, no wonder the rhino isn't scared of the men! With so few rhinos left in the wild, these men are the rhino's only company. I ask if the baby rhino has a name, but Justus just looks at me funny.

**W**e leave the park, cross the border, and drive for a few hours into Tanzania. After dark we pull into a village schoolyard and set up our tents. I drop off still reliving the day's events and sleep a hard, dreamless sleep. In the morning, after packing our tents and making some instant cereal, we get on our bikes. Remembering Justus's advice to stay on the back roads, we turn off the main highway and begin to bike on the red dirt side roads, past small villages and agricultural fields.

In the first few hours, we are stopped five times by huge herds of cattle crossing the road. At first we think the cattle are roaming free. Then we hear someone yelling and see a speck of red in the middle of the herd. A Maasai boy in a red wrap emerges, yelling at

the cattle and hitting their rears with a stick. There are hundreds and hundreds of cows, slowly crossing the road, unconcerned about us. We try to get past by biking in between the cattle, but they have huge horns, and when they look right at us, we back up and bunch together for safety. Finally, we discover that we can use the Pajero to push through the cattle, with Justus honking and driving ahead and us biking along behind.

The red dirt road soon turns into a red dust road, and the dust gets deeper and deeper until it covers the bottom of our bike tires. It feels like biking through five-inch-deep cocoa powder. Thick plumes of the red dust billow up behind me, mixing with my sweat and covering me in a thick coat of red paint. My ears and nostrils are filled with red dust, and I take off my sunglasses, look into the bike's rearview mirror, and gasp. I look like a raccoon, with a red face and white eye patches. Local people walking along the side of the road stare at us. A bus full of Japanese tourists even stops and takes pictures of us, but we keep going, sure that our remote destination will be worth the trip.

As the day wears on, I get tired and fall behind. Reaching the top of a big hill, I look around and don't see any of my teammates. I am so far behind, I am sure I'll never catch up. I know there's nothing I can do but push on, so I start down the hill. Heading toward the bottom, I see a sharp turn and realize I'm going too fast. I try to slow down, but my tires skid on small rocks hidden under the dust and I go flying headfirst over the handlebar, landing with a *poof* in the dust next to the road. I lie still for a moment, mentally assessing my body for damage. *Hmm*, I think, remembering my first disastrous trip on a mountain bike, *this feels familiar.* I don't detect any broken bones or major pain, so I stand up and look for my bike. I groan when I see it, lying in the road, badly twisted. Amazingly, the little stool I got from Chief Tioko is still roped to the rear rack, perfectly intact. I pick up my bike and try to wrench the handlebar back into place. I can't budge it and don't have the right tools to fix it, so the only thing I can do is get back on. I move down the road slowly with a twisted handlebar, a twisted knee, and scraped hands, the bike and I united in a covering of red dust.

It's almost dark when I finally reach the rest of the team, sitting at an intersection in the road next to a shack that sells sodas. At first they look at me as if to say, "Well, where have *you* been?" But as soon as they see my twisted handlebar and frustrated face, they offer me a cool drink and take my bike. After I down the soda and get a wrap on my knee, I learn that we're very close to the camp of the Hadza people. A man named Momoya Muhidoyi, from a nearby village, has offered to take us there.

Rather than getting back on my bike, I call it a day and hop in the Pajero with Justus and Momoya. The rest of the team follows on bikes. We ride along the road for a few miles, and then suddenly, without any warning, the man points off to the right of the road. Justus and I look where he is pointing and see nothing but bushes and open space. There are no trails and no landmarks that we can see to indicate a turnoff, but he keeps pointing and speaking excitedly in Swahili. Justus seems convinced, so he drives right off into the bushes where Momoya is pointing.

As we leave the road, the soil turns soft and

sandy. I look around anxiously, afraid the Pajero will get stuck here in the middle of nowhere. Even the bikers have to dismount and push their bikes through the sand.

After a few minutes of slow going, the ground becomes firmer and starts to head downhill toward a patch of scrubby trees. Ahead on the road, I see a small figure walking, and as we get closer, I see it's a very small man, wearing spotted fur pants with a long spotted tail swinging behind him. Momoya introduces us to Xhaqua (sha-kwa), the leader of the Hadza tribe.

Xhaqua welcomes us by saying, "Mtana." He leads us to a clearing where life seems peaceful. About fifteen men, women, and children are busy at various activities. The men are sitting in one area, leaning against trees, making bows and arrows and smoking tobacco. I watch in amazement as a piece of scrap metal is transformed into a sharp and shiny arrowhead in minutes with only rocks for tools. Sticks are carved, then made into arrows and bent into bows.

A group of women sit with their children around a fire, tending some leftover meat gruel. There's no other food around, but they offer us some. We thank them but say we don't want to take their last bit of food. Also, the meat looks like it's been sitting for a long time. I'm sure my stomach isn't as tough as theirs. I admit to my teammates that I'm afraid of getting sick. The women and children finish the meat and broth and then smash open the jawbone with a rock to suck out the fatty marrow inside.

One of the young girls, a shy twelve-year-old named Boeyacko, shows us around the camp. Boeyacko has a pretty, round face and wears a beaded headband and an old worn kanga, or cloth skirt, that she's sewn together repeatedly with plant fiber thread. I am drawn to this little girl because, when I was young, I dreamed of living out in the wild with animals, sleeping in trees with a pet monkey and gathering things to eat. Boeyacko knows nothing about movie theaters or shopping malls but probably knows a lot about the world around her, how to sew clothes with natural thread, track animals, and make a shelter out of tree branches.

Boeyacko takes us to the small area where the group sleeps. We follow her through an opening in a fence made of thorn bushes that Momoya says protects them from wild animals at night. Boeyacko giggles as she lies down on the ground and pulls a stiff animal skin over herself, pretending to go to sleep. It must be strange for Boeyacko to have a bunch of tourists come into her bedroom and ask all kinds of questions about her life. Can you imagine if someone knocked on your door and asked you how you brush your teeth, talk on the telephone, and do other things that are so normal to you? Finally, Boeyacko shows us her prize possession, a dolly. It's a little figure carved from wood, wrapped in a piece of cloth just like Boeyacko's kanga, and wearing beaded necklaces much like Boeyacko's. Boeyacko holds her dolly like a baby and talks to her in words

I can't understand. She shows her little brother how to hold the dolly properly. Again I'm amazed at how similar Boeyacko is, deep down, to little girls at home.

The men are getting ready for a hunt and say if we give them some money to buy supplies, they will let us come along. To show off their shooting skills, they line up and point to a small plant about a hundred feet away. One after another, they stretch their bows tight and let go with a whoop, each one hitting the plant.

We all agree it would be fascinating to see this small group of men try to hunt gazelles on foot, and they could certainly use money for food and supplies. So we head out, the men in skins in the front and the team behind. We follow their lead, walking slowly and silently, watching and listening for motion or the crack of a twig. After creeping along like this for twenty minutes or so, the men break into a run and fan out, darting around bushes and calling to one another. Then they stop as fast as they start. Whatever they were chasing got away. I never even saw it. I certainly wouldn't survive as a hunter!

We walk along again for a while, more relaxed now, each of us drifting this way and that. I hear a noise in a tangle of vines up in a thorn tree over my head and look up to see a long snake slithering among the thorns. I watch the snake, impressed that it can move through such a thorny tree without getting poked.

A while later, walking along a dry riverbed, a bit apart from the group, I hear a little squeak above and look up to find a tree full of adorable vervet monkeys. They look nervously down at me and then toward the group of men. Their faces are so expressive as they hold the branches with little hands and chatter softly to one another. As I turn to

show the monkeys to the others, the group bursts into action, screaming and running toward another tree.

I jog over just in time to see a Hadza hunter shoot an arrow high into the tree. He hits a monkey. The monkey screams and grabs the arrow, trying to pull it out. The rest of the monkeys are frantic, screeching and jumping from branch to branch. Two run toward the injured one and try to pull out the arrow. I'm crying and want to yell out to make the hunters stop when the monkey falls to the ground and lies still. I can't stand to watch, so I walk away.

Struggling not to judge the hunters, I keep my distance from them all the way back.

When I arrive at camp, the monkey is already cooking and the group is excited. When the meat is done, they grab it from the fire and pull it apart. I think, *These people are barbaric, eating a little creature that was alive and chattering with its brothers and sisters only minutes ago.* I want to teach them about monkeys and how smart and social they are.

Then I look over as one of the hunters calls to one of the dogs. The dog comes over with its tail wagging, and the hunter pets the dog and feeds it a piece of meat. I am amazed. There is so little meat for the whole group, and the man is taking care of the dog! It is the first time in Africa that I have seen a dog so unafraid and a person treating it so well, almost like a part of the family. It reminds me of my dog and makes me miss my home. I look down and bite my lip to keep from getting sad. When I look up at the group again, it seems so different. Not barbarians, but friends and family. A father feeding his little girl, two young women talking and giggling while they relish the food. I realize we aren't so different after all.

Later I ask Momoya if it bothers the Hadza to kill a smart creature like a monkey. "Not really," he says. "But they'd prefer to kill a bigger animal like a kudu or an impala that will provide more meat. They eat a lot of monkeys now because so many people are moving in, hunting with guns, and scaring off the larger wild animals with their cattle."

I realize that the kudu and the Hazda are both endangered. They have the same enemy: the modern world and farmers and ranchers who are moving in to take over the Hazda's land. It's not that I'm against modernizing. Actually, I think the Hazda will adapt to the changes. I'm not so sure about the kudu. I wish all could somehow survive.

# 7. Wild Animal Soup!

We say good-bye to Momoya, Xhaqua, Boeyacko, and the rest of the Hadza group, who watch us pack up and set out on our bikes. Once we push through the sand to a dirt road, the going gets a little easier and the scrubby vegetation becomes grassier and more open. We have a long day of riding ahead of us, but we are excited; by the end of the day we'll finally reach the long-awaited Ngorongoro Crater.

Though it's better than the sand, the road is rough at first, with rocks and potholes that threaten to bounce me right off my bike. It takes all my concentration, watching the road ahead, to avoid this rock on the right and that pothole on the left. Sometimes my wheel or foot hits a big rock and I yelp out loud. At last we turn onto the main road, a small highway that has no rocks or potholes and even has a bit of extra pavement on the side. What a relief! Now I can look around me and am surprised to see grass, as far as the eye can see. It's the African savanna I've been waiting for! Still, I don't see the big herds of wildlife I've imagined for so long. Now, more than ever, I wonder if my vision of a wild Africa teeming with animals is just a fantasy. Well, there should be lots of animals at Ngorongoro Crater, but it's so flat here, it's hard to imagine we'll be amid mountains and volcanic craters by the end of the day. Frustrated, I say, "So, where are these volcanoes? I don't even see any evidence of volcanoes here."

Hearing my own voice say "evidence of volcanoes" triggers something I learned from my early research on the Rift Valley. Of course! The grasslands are the evidence of volcanoes. In fact, the grasslands and most of the wildlife wouldn't even exist here if it weren't for volcanoes.

Millions of years ago, there were so many eruptions that all of East Africa was covered in a thick layer of ash. Every time it rained, the ash formed a hard layer like concrete, so hard that tree roots couldn't penetrate. But grasses with shallow roots could take hold, so enormous grasslands formed. All the grass attracted huge herds of grazing animals, and the grazers attracted predators like lions, cheetahs, and hyenas. Eventually, some trees pushed through, providing food for other types of animals like giraffes and elephants.

Over time the animals have learned to live together by sharing food. The impala eat the tips and stalks of the tall grass, making way for tender new shoots to sprout up, which are eaten by tiny antelopes called dik-diks.

Giraffes can reach tall vegetation when food on the ground is scarce, and elephants can eat the toughest bark and thorns. In the process of tearing off bark and branches, elephants push over trees, helping to keep the grassland from turning into a forest.

Eating different parts of grass and trees helps all these animals live together on the same land.

I've been so focused on my thoughts about the savanna ecosystem that once again I look up and am startled by my surroundings. It seems that all of a sudden a large mountain range looms in front of us. It looks dark and dense, in contrast with the dun-colored savanna all around us. In order to arrive before dark, we load up our bikes and cram into the Pajero.

As we start to climb rapidly up into the foothills, we leave the dry grass and occasional thorn tree of the savanna far below. We wind up a steep dirt road, past acacia forests, then farther on up through thicker forests with big, green leaves, and finally into wet forests with dripping moss hanging from tree branches. It's so cool and wet and green, almost like the rain forests I've visited in South America. I can't believe I'm still in Africa! Just an hour ago, the sun was beating on me, my throat was dry, and sweat was trickling down my face. Now the air is so cool and moist, I lean out the window to get a refreshing burst of air. As we near the rim, the ground slopes even more steeply and the road doubles back and forth in switchbacks. I'm looking ahead, eagerly anticipating the first glimpse into the crater. What will I see first—some zebra, wildebeest, or maybe a rhino?

We round a hairpin turn and find ourselves face-to-face with a group of Cape buffalo! Each one is as big as a car, and they just stand and stare right at us, unwilling to move. I know they are very dangerous and could charge our jeep, maybe even flip it, but I can't help giggling when I look at them. To me their horns look like funny wigs.

A little farther on, we startle a couple of big old elephants in the road and stop the car. Many animals climb up the steep sides of Ngorongoro Mountain and down into Ngorongoro Crater, mainly to drink water from the lake, which is the only year-round source of water for many miles. These elephants seem tired, as if they've been walking a long way. Justus also points out that they're males and they have really fat tusks, which means they're old. Justus tells us that, in addition to going for water, old male elephants

make their last migration to the bottom of the crater to "retire." As their teeth wear down, elephants can't eat their usual food, so they go to the crater to finish their days eating the soft yellow bark of a special type of acacia tree that grows there. He adds that we won't see any elephant family groups in the crater because the crater walls are too steep for the very young elephants. We start the car again and the elephants flap their ears and disappear into the forest.

Now that we've seen these animals, I'm ready for more. My eyes are peeled and I have my whole body leaning out of the window to see farther ahead. Around another corner I hear loud squeals and catch a glimpse of a wild boar as it snorts, squeals, and rustles off into the bush. With all the noise boars make, I am not surprised to learn that a group of them is called a sounder of boars.

Climbing over the lip and looking into Ngorongoro Crater, I am stunned. All I read couldn't have prepared me for the sight. Standing on the rim, I look down and out over a huge expanse of forest, grassland, and the lake, all within a giant bowl. I see dark areas on the savanna, like huge shadows, and realize they are enormous herds, thousands and thousands of zebras, wildebeest, and Cape buffalo. I can't see them, but I know where there are grazers there are predators: lions, cheetahs, hyenas, and leopards. It's hard to imagine that some of the tiny specks are as big as a car. Looking out over the entire crater, it looks to me like a giant bowl of animal soup!

The road tumbles down from the rim at a steep pitch, clinging to the sides of the crater and zigzagging back and forth. As we wind carefully down, around potholes and eroded areas, it feels as if the Pajero, with its heavy load, might just topple over, so we lean to one side of the truck, toward the crater wall. Justus jams on the brakes, and we all look up, startled. A troupe of baboons is crossing the road in front of us! Across, they climb up onto a small hill and calmly watch us pass. As we drive by, I have to laugh. A tiny baby baboon is sitting straight up on its mother's back, looking as excited to see us as we are to see it!

As we drive down closer to the crater floor, the specks get bigger and bigger, more and more real. I feel chills of excitement and a slight fear as we continue driving right toward the huge, solid herd of animals. When we reach the crater floor, the Pajero is literally stopped in traffic, only the obstacles are not other cars but countless wildebeest, Cape buffalo, zebra, and gazelles. I look around and realize I'm right in the middle of what's called a "mixed herd," animals that group together to help one another survive. For instance, zebras have better vision and hearing than wildebeest, so they give an early warning when a predator is near. And wildebeest are apparently tastier to predators, so zebras are less likely to be attacked when they stick close to wildebeest. I've read so much about mixed herds. Now I am seeing them for real!

As we push slowly through the huge herd, a baby wildebeest is separated from its mother.

The mother and baby make mooing sounds to each other, frantically trying to reunite. When we pass by, there is a moment when I am right between the baby and mother as they search and finally see each other through the windows of our jeep. For that moment I have the thrilling feeling that I am somehow part of their communication, part of their world. Maybe if I stayed long enough, I could learn their language!

I don't know if it's the heat of all the animals or the intense African sun, but suddenly the Pajero feels like a frying pan; even the doors are hot to the touch. We decide to explore the shady forest at the edge of the crater. The instant we leave the hot open grassland, we feel relief. We drive to a clearing just inside the trees and find, to our delight, a whole group of vervet monkeys sitting on a fallen branch!

First I feel sad, thinking of the monkey that the Hadza hunters shot, but watching the monkeys' crazy antics, I start laughing out loud. I'm laughing so much that I can't get a good photo, so I get out my beanbag, a little pillow filled with dried beans or rice many photographers use to steady their cameras, and put it on the roof of the Pajero.

I am standing with my head out the window, watching the monkeys jump and wrestle on the log. I watch so intently that I don't notice one of them creeping through the grass toward us. Before I know it, there is a monkey on the roof rack, right beside me! He looks me right in the face, grabs the bean-bag, and takes a flying leap off the back of the Pajero! Then, just to rub it in, he stops fifteen feet away and stares at me again as he rips into the bag and stuffs beans in his mouth.

Well, apparently, vervet monkeys don't like dried pinto beans, because the monkey instantly spits out every one. Another monkey runs up, arms and tail flying every which way, screams, grabs the beans, and shoves some in his mouth. But he makes a surprised face and spits them out, too. When Justus opens the door of the truck, the monkeys run away, leaving the beans behind. When I get the beanbag back, there are holes all over it from the monkeys' teeth. *Yikes!* I think. *That could have been my hand.* As if that isn't enough, when I'm not looking, the monkey runs back, jumps up on the roof again, and pees all over it.

Just then another vehicle full of tourists on safari drives into the clearing and spots the monkeys. A woman climbs up on the roof and throws them a sandwich. No wonder the monkeys are so bold. They probably get fed all the time! I'm not upset at the monkey anymore, but I want to yell at the woman and tell her that she will be responsible for a dead monkey when one gets shot for being a pest.

We only have a couple of hours before the road closes, and we've only seen part of the crater. We decide to head to the lake to see if there are any hippos or flamingos there. But we don't get far before someone yells, "Lion!"

I strain to see a lion, but all I see is grass. Then I notice a puffy piece of grass moving differently from the rest that's blowing in the wind. It's flicking back and forth with no particular rhythm. It's the lion's tail! Strange, the motion reminds me of something I've seen before. That irritated flick . . . ? That's it! When I used to bother my cat at home, trying to pet her too much or staring at her, she got annoyed at me and flicked her tail like that. It looks exactly the same.

We drive a little bit closer, and I pull out my binoculars. Up close I can see the tail distinctly, and follow it back down toward the . . . Whoa! A huge head rises up and swings around, and I almost drop my binoculars.

A regal face with intelligent, almond-shaped eyes, a long, straight nose, and thick mane looks right at me. I freeze, wondering if we've gotten too close, but before we can move, the lion flops back down and resumes his tail flicking.

"He's huge!" I exclaim.

"Yes, he eats a lot and sleeps sometimes twenty hours a day," Justus tells us. "And watch out if his tail starts to jerk up and down. That means he's about to charge."

We wait around for over an hour, but the lion doesn't do anything, just lounges in the grass, flicking his tail back and forth. It starts to get dark, so finally we decide to continue our search for hippos and flamingos.

Just minutes later someone yells, "Big Bird!"

"Very funny," I say. "Big Bird wouldn't stand a chance out here. He can't even fly." I turn to look, and indeed there is a huge bird in front of us. It's an ostrich, and it's starting to run! The eight-foot-tall bird starts to trot, then ruffles its feathers and speeds off, pumping its legs. "She can run more than thirty miles an hour," Justus reminds us.

"That's fast!" I say. "Wait a minute, why did you say *she*?" I ask Justus, grinning. It's a pet peeve of mine that whenever people see an animal, they always call it a he, whether it is or not.

"See that other one over there, on the nest?" Justus points back to where we first saw the ostrich. We squint our eyes, looking out onto the darkening savanna. Finally, I spot a big, dark shape on the ground.

"Wow! That's well camouflaged!"

"Yes, that's the point," Justus tells me. "The male is black, so he sits on the nest at night; and the female is light-colored, so she sits during the day."

"Cool!" I exclaim. "But of course the female still gets the hard job, sitting in the hot sun all day."

Justus laughs; I knew he would.

Suddenly, we realize it's getting really dark

out and if we don't get back fast, we might get stuck in the crater for the night, with no food. Quickly, we change plans and head straight back toward the road.

On our way out of the crater, I catch a glimpse of bright red amid the deep grass and animals. It's the bright red shawl of a Maasai herdsman who has walked all the way down from the rim to water his cattle at the lake. Justus tells me that the Maasai have been using the lake for so long that the crater was named for the sound of their cows' bells ringing *ga-dong, ga-dong, ga-dong* as the cows go up and down. When "Ngorongoro" is pronounced properly, it does sound sort of like bells: "in-GA-dong-GA-do." I watch the Maasai lead his cattle, weaving his way through the herds of wildebeest and Cape buffalo, and wonder how he stays safe. I imagine myself walking through the herd, not having a clue how to tell if an animal is about to charge me. I look at the Maasai man with awe, thinking, *Now there is someone who is truly immersed in the natural world and really under-stands its various languages.*

I think of Justus and his stories of growing up in the Turkana village, herding goats as a young boy. I marvel at how differently he spends his day now, working in a fossil museum in the huge city of Nairobi. In his lifetime he has seen such contrast. He knows the joys and hardships of village life from a childhood spent dancing, singing, and work-ing with his father's herds. Because of his experiences, he can understand the world of a Maasai herdsman, but he can also understand my more modern world, going to school and getting around in a city. The Maasai herdsman and I have no common experience. I cannot imagine what goes on in his mind, nor can he imagine what goes on in mine. But we both enjoy being here.

As we drive out of the crater, I have a feel-ing of nostalgia, a fear that maybe the next time I'm able to come back, many of the things I've seen will be gone, having given way to modern society. Lost in this sad thought, I am jolted awake when the Pajero hits a big rock and swerves toward the steep bank down into the crater. Justus flashes me a big smile and says, "It can be fine!" I realize right then that if Justus, who has lived here his whole life, believes things can be fine, then they can be. The cultures and wildlife of Africa have been around a long, long time. Change is part of life, and though sometimes we don't want things to change, we can't put the world in a bubble.

The next day we are headed back to Nairobi, and though the nostalgia is still there, I feel very happy and calm. I finally got to see the Africa of my dreams, to experience a sea of animals with very few people, the way the world must have been hundreds of years ago. Finding myself amid thousands of animals, looking into the eyes of a wildebeest, and feeling the instinctual bond between mother and baby will stay with me forever. I already realize how much this trip has changed me. I started this journey focused only on the plight of wildlife, blaming people for their decline. But I learned that the cultures of Africa are also threatened by the spread of modern society. The people I've met have inspired me tremendously—Justus, Chief Tioko, Jason Hassrick, Shirley Strum, and the others who are meeting Africa's challenges with energy and optimism. Their love for the people and animals of Africa gives me hope that they, and others like them, will somehow be able to find solutions.

When we're finally back at the airport, Justus waits with us for the plane. I wish he would just go, because looking at his eyes get watery and hearing him ask when we're coming back is too hard. I promise I'll come back as soon as I can, but we both know it may be many years. As soon as I step on the plane, my eyes well up and I start to think of all the things I wish I'd left with Justus—my bike, my panniers, my watch. As I cram my panniers into the overhead compartment,

Chief Tioko's stool pops out, making me smile as I remember all the miles I rode with it strapped on the back of my bike. I sit down in my seat, suddenly exhausted. I look out the window and catch one last glimpse of Justus, waving madly and smiling. As the plane rolls down the runway, my mind is full of people, animals, and overwhelming emotion. We take off, and the last image I have before I drift into dreams of Africa is the huge swath of protected land right next to the city that is Nairobi National Park. Giraffes next to skyscrapers. Anything is possible.

# More About the Animals

# Zebras!

**Common Name:** Plains zebra
**Swahili Name:** *punda milia*
**Scientific Name:** *Equus burchelli*
**Name of Group:** Herd or crossing of zebras
**Closest Relative:** Horse
**Dietary Classification:** Herbivore
**Favorite Food:** Grass
**Weight:** Adults weigh up to 750 pounds.
**Life Span:** Up to twenty years
**Litter Size:** Usually one foal
**Worst Enemies:** Lions, hyenas, crocodiles, and humans
**Best Defense:** Flight whenever possible, but if cornered, stallions kick backward with their hind legs.
**Sounds:** Whinnies, neighs, brays, and snorts (much like horse sounds)
**Preferred Habitat:** Light woodland and savannas

### Fun Facts:

- Another type of zebra, called the Grevy's zebra, is much more rare, lives in drier habitats, and has thinner stripes than the Plains zebra.
- Strangely enough, zebra stripes are camouflage against predators. This type of camouflage is called disruptive coloration because the stripes make zebras difficult for predators to see among the grass and long shadows at dawn and dusk.
- Zebras' excellent hearing and eyesight help alert them to predators like lions and hyenas. This "predator alarm" also helps other animals that tend to herd with zebras, such as wildebeest and antelopes.

# Ticks!

**Common Name:** Ticks
**Swahili Name:** *papasi*
**Scientific Name:** 70 species in Kenya alone,
*Boophilus spp.* and *Rhipicephalus spp.*, for example
**Name of Group:** Swarm or flock of ticks
**Closest Relative:** Spider
**Dietary Classification:** Sanguivore
**Favorite Food:** Blood!
**Weight:** Varies among species, but a tick may increase its body weight up to a hundred times when it fills up on blood.
**Life Span:** Some ticks can live up to twenty years.
**Litter Size:** An adult female can produce up to 20,000 eggs.
**Worst Enemies:** People armed with tweezers and insect repellent
**Best Defense:** Being small, firmly attached, and hard to spot
**Sound:** A sucking sound too quiet for human ears
**Preferred Habitat:** Fields and forests with mammals

### Fun Facts:

- There are some 850 species of ticks in the world. Most ticks specialize on a particular type of animal, for example, reptiles, birds, or mammals (including people!).
- To find their next meal, juvenile ticks climb up plants, wave their front legs in the air, and wait for warm blood to walk by. Ticks can sense vibration, a shadow, a change in the carbon dioxide level, or a temperature change. Ticks are antigravitational, which means that they can move upward from wherever they latch on and keep going until they reach a barrier, where they begin to feed.
- While they are feeding, ticks excrete saliva, mixed with any bacteria or viruses they are carrying, into the host's bloodstream. Certain types of ticks transmit serious diseases, like Lyme disease or Rocky Mountain spotted fever.

# Dung Beetles!

**Common Name:** Dung beetle
**Swahili Name:** *dundu*
**Scientific Name:** *Scarabeus sacer*
**Name of Group:** Dung beetles are not usually found in groups, but when beetles in general are in a big group, it is called a swarm.
**Closest Relatives:** Japanese beetle and June bug
**Dietary Classification:** Detritivore
**Favorite Foods:** Animal dung and other decomposing material
**Length:** Two to fifty millimeters
**Life Span:** Two years or more
**Litter Size:** A single egg in each dung ball; each female produces only about 20 eggs in her lifetime.
**Worst Enemies:** Baboons, monitor lizards, and owls
**Best Defenses:** Rolling up in a ball, hissing
**Sounds:** Dung beetles make creaky, scratchy, or chirping sounds by "stridulating," rubbing their head against the hard shell covering their upper back, or by rubbing their body against something like a rock or tree bark. They make these sounds when they are threatened, and male dung beetles may "sing" to attract females to their dung heap! Unfortunately, the sounds are usually too soft for humans to hear.
**Preferred Habitat:** Savannas with lots of big mammals

### Fun Facts:

- There are over seven thousand types of dung beetles in the world!
- Dung beetles have different strategies for finding poop. Some types march alongside herds of animals, waiting for the poop to fall; others fly after herds of animals; and yet others just sit and wait in strategic spots, like game trails, for stinky odors to waft by their sensitive noses.
- Dung beetles also have different strategies for "working" the poop. One type, known as "rollers," makes perfectly round balls of dung (up to fifty times their own weight) and rolls them far away from the dung pile.

# Hippos!

**Common Name:** Hippopotamus
**Swahili Name:** *kiboko*
**Scientific Name:** *Hippopotamus amphibius*
**Name of Group:** Bloat of hippos
**Closest Relative:** Pig
**Dietary Classification:** Herbivore
**Favorite Food:** Grass—up to 150 pounds a day!
**Weight:** Up to three and a half tons
**Life Span:** Up to forty-two years in the wild
**Litter Size:** One calf
**Worst Enemies:** Humans, lions, crocodiles, and hyenas
**Best Defenses:** Trampling, biting, or goring with teeth
**Sounds:** *"MUH-muh-muh"* for dominance, high-pitched neighs if attacked, and snorts underwater
**Preferred Habitat:** Rivers, lakes, and swamps

## Fun Facts:

- Hippos will fight fiercely to protect their babies, sometimes even killing big crocodiles in their massive jaws.
- Hippos' eyes and ears are located on top of their heads so they can see and hear without leaving the water. When they go underwater, they can close their nostrils and ears to be completely watertight. Still, hippos are not good swimmers and prefer to leap or hop along the bottom.
- Hippos have special flat tails ringed with bristles that they may flap back and forth while they poop, splattering their dung all around. Scientists are not sure about the purpose of this "muck-spreading." Some think it is territorial, while others believe it is a way of marking the hippos' path to the water.

# Elephants!

**Common Name:** African elephant
**Swahili Name:** *tembo* or *ndovu*
**Scientific Name:** *Loxodonta africana*
**Name of Group:** Herd of elephants
**Closest Relative:** Florida manatee
**Dietary Classification:** Herbivore
**Favorite Foods:** Grass, bark, and leaves
**Weight:** At three and a half to six and a half tons,
it's the largest living land mammal.
**Life Span:** Average sixty to seventy years
**Litter Size:** One calf
**Worst Enemies:** Humans
**Best Defenses:** Run away (up to twenty-two miles per hour!) or
charge, trample, and gore with tusks
**Sounds:** Trumpeting, squealing, low-frequency calls we can't hear
**Preferred Habitat:** From tropical rain forests to savannas

### Fun Facts:

- An elephant's trunk, which is actually an elongated nose and upper lip, has no bones, but consists of forty thousand bundles of longitudinal and circular muscles. They enable the six- to seven-foot-long trunk to delicately pick up a blade of grass and gently caress a family member, or violently pull over an entire tree.
- Elephants' trunks can be like hands. Elephants sometimes greet each other and "hug" by wrapping their trunks together. Baby elephants often suck their trunks like thumbs for comfort.
- Many low-frequency elephant sounds travel over long distances, to individuals or herds that are up to two miles away.

# Lions!

**Common Name:** *Lion*
**Swahili Name:** *simba*
**Scientific Name:** *Panthera leo*
**Name of Group:** Pride of lions
**Closest Relative:** Mountain lion
**Dietary Classification:** Carnivore
**Favorite Foods:** Wildebeest, zebras, and other animals
**Weight:** Males average 400 pounds, and females average 260. This great difference between the weight of male and female is called sexual dimorphism.
**Life Span:** Up to twenty-five years in captivity, twelve to fifteen in the wild
**Litter Size:** Two to four cubs
**Worst Enemies:** Humans, leopards, and hyenas
**Best Defenses:** Run, hide, or attack!
**Sounds:** Roars, purrs, and moans
**Preferred Habitat:** Savannas with lots of prey animals

### Fun Facts:

- Female lions do almost all the hunting, while the males sleep, up to twenty hours a day! Lions hunt in packs to ambush their prey because most of their prey run faster than a lion's maximum speed of thirty-seven miles per hour.
- Lions used to live all over Africa and Europe.
- A pride of lions is made up of related females (daughters, mothers, and grandmothers) who cooperate to do almost all the hunting. Still, when they make a kill, they wait for the males to eat first.

# Hyenas!

**Common Name:** Spotted hyena
**Swahili Name:** *fisi*
**Scientific Name:** *Crocuta crocuta*
**Name of Group:** Cackle or clan of hyenas
**Closest Relative:** Mongoose. Though they look more like dogs, hyenas are actually more closely related to cats.
**Dietary Classification:** Carnivore
**Favorite Foods:** Preferably fresh zebra, wildebeest, gazelle, topi, or buffalo. Hyenas are primarily hunters, not scavengers, but will eat carrion (rotting meat) if fresh meat isn't available.
**Weight:** Unlike most mammals that show sexual dimorphism, female hyenas are larger than males, with a maximum weight of 165 pounds, as compared to the males' maximum weight of 140.
**Life Span:** Hyenas live up to twenty-five years in captivity, but in the wild their life span is much shorter—an average of twelve years.
**Litter Size:** One to four cubs, average two
**Worst Enemies:** Humans
**Best Defense:** Attacking in packs
**Sound:** Cackling
**Preferred Habitat:** Savannas

### Fun Facts:

- Legends in many African cultures depict hyenas as evil creatures associated with and ridden by witches. The well-known cackling of hyenas, which many people think makes the hyena sound evil, is actually a social call that can be heard up to three miles away, telling the rest of the clan to come share in a successful hunt.
- Though they have an awkward-looking, loping gait, hyenas can run up to thirty miles per hour for several miles.
- Hyenas are bold hunters, contrary to their reputation as cowards. Hyenas have even been known on occasion to attack humans. Humans have in turn eaten hyenas, after domesticating them and fattening them up.

133

# Baboons!

**Common Name:** Olive baboon
**Swahili Name:** *nyani*
**Scientific Name:** *Papio anubis*
**Name of Group:** Troop of baboons
**Closest Relatives:** Other baboon and primate species
**Dietary Classification:** Mainly frugivorous, but also opportunistic
**Favorite Foods:** Subsist mainly on fruits, but also take whatever's available, from plant roots to leaves to insects and small mammals
**Weight:** Females up to 40 pounds, males up to 90 pounds; another great example of sexual dimorphism
**Life Span:** Twenty to thirty years
**Litter Size:** One offspring
**Worst Enemies:** Leopards, lions, and humans
**Best Defenses:** Large teeth, ability to attack as a pack
**Sounds:** A huge "vocabulary," from barks to warn of predators, roaring during fights, and clicking, which is a submissive call made by young baboons
**Preferred Habitat:** Savannas and woodlands

## Fun Facts:

- Baboons can survive for a long period without water by licking the morning dew from their fur.
- In baboon body language, lip-smacking is a way baboons reassure each other that everything is okay.
- When confronted by a leopard or cheetah, baboons will try to appear threatening and may attack as a mob, often severely wounding the predator.

# Camels!

**Common Name:** Dromedary camel
**Swahili Name:** *ngamia*
**Scientific Name:** *Camelus dromedarius*
**Name of Group:** Flock, train, or caravan of camels
**Closest Relative:** Llama
**Dietary Classification:** Herbivore
**Favorite Foods:** Leaves and grasses, but able to eat practically anything that grows in the desert, including salty plants rejected by other grazers
**Weight:** Adults up to 1600 pounds
**Life Span:** Forty years
**Litter Size:** One calf
**Worst Enemies:** Humans, who may eat camel meat!
**Best Defenses:** Kicking, biting, spitting
**Sounds:** Loud groaning and belching
**Preferred Habitat:** Deserts

## Fun Facts:

- Contrary to the popular belief that a camel stores water in its hump, a camel's hump is mostly fat! The lump of fat serves as an energy store when there is little to eat. In addition, having all their fat on their back instead of spread over their bodies helps camels stay cool in the desert heat.

- The knifelife shape of their bodies also helps them stay cool. They can turn toward the sun to minimize the solar heat and radiation they soak up, while their wide flat sides, with millions of capillaries just below the skin surface, emit heat.

- Even a camel's hair, which is shiny and reflective and can stand up like goose bumps, helps keep a camel up to ninety degrees cooler than surface air temperatures!

# A Note from the Author

In classrooms across America, over three million kids followed AfricaQuest on the Internet. You may be curious to know how we hooked up to the web out in the wilds of Africa! We had a relatively small satellite dish and a special terminal that allowed us to connect our laptops to the Internet. The dish could be broken into pieces and put into our bike panniers if needed, but most of the time it rode in the vehicle and met up with us each night. It amazed me that we could get electronically linked to the outside world—while hippos were crunching and snorting right near our tents! We were able to send our reports, photos, and videos to Classroom Connect, Inc., in San Francisco and download questions we got from kids every night. The students also voted on which location we would travel to next—so it's thanks to them that we saw such interesting places! (For more information about AfricaQuest, visit www.harperchildrens.com and go to *Hippos in the Night*.)

After much thinking about the focus of the book, I realized that it would be impossible to talk in-depth about logistics of the trip—as well as my teammates and the way we worked together—without detracting from the focus on Africa and the animals and people I became acquainted with there. I am indebted to my wonderful teammates, who made AfricaQuest such an exciting adventure, and feel honored to have known each of them. I would like especially to acknowledge a few who, directly or indirectly, helped make this book possible—Dan Buettner for his original vision and unstoppable can-do attitude, John Fox for his friendship and adherence to educational excellence, Beth Wald for her stunning photos and commitment to seeing the book to completion, and Justus Erus for his optimism and unflagging sense of humor. Thank you.